COOKING & EATING

BY ROBIN TWIDDY

BookLife
PUBLISHING

BookLife Publishing Ltd.
King's Lynn
Norfolk PE30 4LS

Printed in Malaysia.

A catalogue record for this book is available from the British Library.

ISBN: 9781-78637-626-8

Written by:
Robin Twiddy

Edited by:
Madeline Tyler

Designed by:
Gareth Liddington

Photocredits: All images are courtesy of Shutterstock.com.

Cover – morkovkapiy, Rawpixel.com, kurhan, donatas1205, 2 – Andrey_Popov, 4 – maradon 333, GaudiLab, Mangostar, 5 – karamysh, andersphoto, Gary Perkin, 6 – MikeBiTa, NATHAPON KWIANWONG, 7 – James Puckett, 8 – Ulf Wittrock, 9 – Internet Archive Book Images, 10 – Internet Archive Book Images, 11 – Rawpixel.com, 12 – narai chai, Monkey Business Images, 13 – Nasky, Designua, 14 – Dmitry Bodyaev, showcake, 15 – Amelia Martin, RoJo Images, 16 – Cemre, Wolfmann, 17 – ThongPooN, Yellow Cat, 18 – DuxX, 19 – Evikka, anucha maneechote, Ahanov Michael, 20 – Atlaspix, 21 – Sergey Nemirovsky, vitalikaladdin, 22 – industryviews, RomboStudio, 23 – Fae Hartsook, 24 – Stockr, Alf Ribeiro, 25 – Nejron Photo, Winston Link, 26 – Kondor83, 27 – Sorbis, Syda Productions, 28 – Denys Prykhodov, Viktor Kochetkov, Sapunova Svetlana, 29 – Georgejmclittle, Dragon Images, 30 – MarinaGrigorivna.

Images are courtesy of Shutterstock.com. With thanks to Getty Images, Thinkstock Photo and iStockphoto.

CONTENTS

Words that look like <u>this</u> are explained in the glossary on page 31.

HOW CAN MACHINES CHANGE THE WORLD?

Food – we all need it to survive. But did you know that our relationship with food has changed the world and shaped us as a species? From the first tools made from stone over two million years ago, used to kill animals and prepare the meat, to the development of agriculture by the people of the Stone Age, our future has always been tied to the food we eat and how we get that food.

YOU ARE WHAT YOU EAT

From simple machines to complex inventions, technology and machinery can solve problems, make life easier, and change society. Understanding the everyday machines we take for granted can help us understand the world around us a little better. Do you ever really think about where your food comes from? How it gets to you? Or, what is happening inside your microwave?

Why do we invent new things? We invent new machines to solve problems! And of course, when a new machine solves a big problem, then it has the potential to change the world. Some of the machines that have changed the world are in your kitchens, inside your cupboards and even under your sinks.

Sometimes the technology used in one machine can lead to the creation of a completely different machine. Did you know that the steam engine was first used to help miners in Spain, but later changed the world when it was used on the railways? Inventions like these can lead to huge changes in society.

Steam Engine used in a Cornish Tin Mine

STEAM ENGINE TO TRAINS!

KEEPING IT COLD

WHY FREEZE FOOD?

People have known for thousands of years that you can preserve food by freezing it. However, it was only in the 20th century that technology allowed people to do this at home without keeping a cellar full of snow or ice.

In ancient China, people kept ice in their cellars to use in the summer.

Rotting Carrots

KEEP IT COOL!

Food rots because of the bacteria that grows on it. Lots of things affect how quickly this process happens, such as air, light, moisture and temperature. By reducing the temperature of the food, we can slow the growth of bacteria. Refrigerators keep food cool, but they also control light and air flow too.

Freezing foods does not make it unhealthy.

ENTER THE REFRIGERATOR

The development of the refrigerator and the freezer go hand in hand, but the humble refrigerator arrived first. Beginning with experiments in the late 18th century and the early 19th century, people tried all sorts of ways to control temperature. However, it wasn't until 1914 that we saw the first electric refrigerator for the home.

Early electric refrigerators had some serious drawbacks. First, you needed to have an air compressor and a motor installed into your kitchen. These fridges used dangerous <u>chemicals</u> placed in a <u>vacuum</u> to create ice. A leaking fridge often didn't end well for the owner. 1920 saw the introduction of Freon, a safer alternative to the chemicals used before.

This is an advertisement for the Kelvinator, one of the first safe domestic refrigerators.

IF YOU CAN'T STAND THE HEAT, GET OUT OF THE KITCHEN

COOKING IN THE HOME

Being able to cook hot meals at home has always been important for families and communities. From cooking meals on an open fire to the modern cooker, the way we prepare meals has been changed by the technology available. The ancient Greeks invented ovens to bake bread, and people in the Middle Ages used hearths with chimneys, and cooked in cauldrons.

It was the 19th century that really saw a revolution in cooking technology as gas and electricity became available in homes. Before this, the home oven changed lots of times, from wood burning, to coal and kerosene. But these types of fuel were messy and smelly. Gas and electricity were neither messy nor smelly.

Later, wood and coal burning stoves were often made from cast iron, making them very heavy.

NOW YOU'RE COOKING WITH GAS

James Sharp introduced England to the first commercial gas stove in the early 1800s. However, it took a long time for it to take off. Early gas stoves needed to be lit with a match and could be very dangerous if there was a build-up of gas in the stove. Horror stories of a neighbour blowing themselves up when making dinner might put you off buying one!

If you smell gas in your home or school you should tell someone because it could be dangerous.

WHY GAS?

There are lots of benefits to cooking with gas. A lot of professional kitchens use gas because they can provide instant heat, an even spread of heat across a pan and more control of that heat than an electric or wood stove.

HOW DOES IT WORK?

- Gas is fed to the cooker from the gas mains.
- Turning the control knobs opens a valve, releasing the gas through the hob jets.
- Either turning the control knob or pressing the starter button triggers an electric circuit, producing a spark.
- The spark ignites the gas, creating a flame around the burner.

EX-STATIC ABOUT ELECTRICITY

The electric stove was invented by William Hadaway in 1896. However, it didn't become a standard in the home until the 1920s. When Hadaway invented it, very few homes had electricity. In 1906, David Curle Smith made an electric oven that would become the basis for most modern cookers: a main oven and a top oven with four hobs on top.

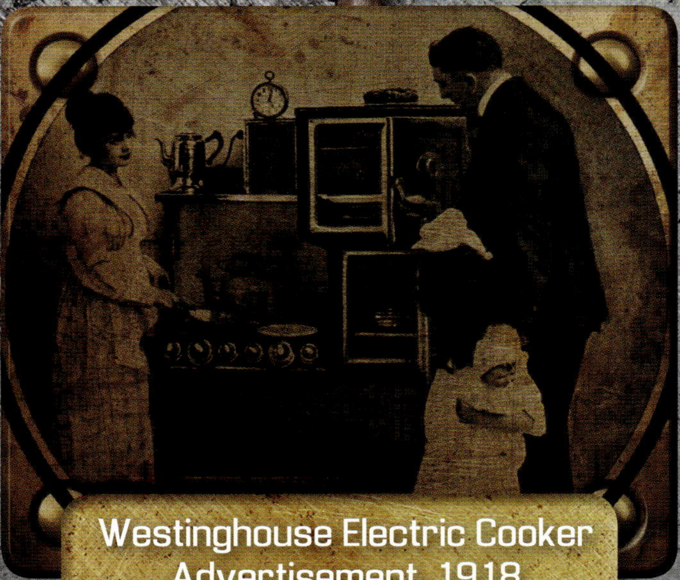

Westinghouse Electric Cooker Advertisement, 1918

Some ovens can be hotter at the top than at the bottom. Others have a fan which distributes the heat.

HOW DOES IT WORK?

The modern electric oven works in the same basic way today as they did over 100 years ago. Electric ovens are pretty simple machines. When you switch the oven on, electricity runs through and heats a coiled wire inside an element. This then heats the surrounding air, and a fan then circulates this hot air.

CLEVER OVEN

The electric oven does something very clever when it heats up. The heating element cycles on and off to maintain the temperature at which it is set. This is controlled by a thermostat that is constantly monitoring the temperature inside the oven.

WHAT THE OVEN DID FOR US

Whether you have an electric or gas oven, this machine has changed the way people eat in their homes. Thanks to the modern oven, people can cook with ease without needing to have fuel such as coal or wood always at hand.

MICROWAVE

A LUCKY ACCIDENT

Believe it or not, the microwave oven, which is now found in many kitchens across the world, was created by accident. Percy Spencer had worked on radar technology, which uses microwaves, during the Second World War. After the war ended, Spencer was trying to find a new way to use his microwave technology. It was then that he noticed the chocolate bar in his pocket had melted! One sticky pocket was the inspiration for the microwave oven.

Radio Tower

WHY IS THE MICROWAVE OVEN IMPORTANT?

Once the technology had been mastered and made better, it quickly became popular. The microwave oven doesn't need to heat up before use, so it saves electricity, and heats food more quickly than an ordinary oven. Most importantly, it opened up a whole new food market – the microwave meal.

The first available microwave oven was almost two metres tall!

The big drawback of microwaves is that they are harmful to living cells. This is why microwave ovens have a metal box around them; it stops the microwaves from escaping. When it is turned on, a device called a magnetron transforms the electricity into powerful radio waves. These waves blast the food passing through and causing the molecules in the food to vibrate. These vibrations create heat which cooks the food.

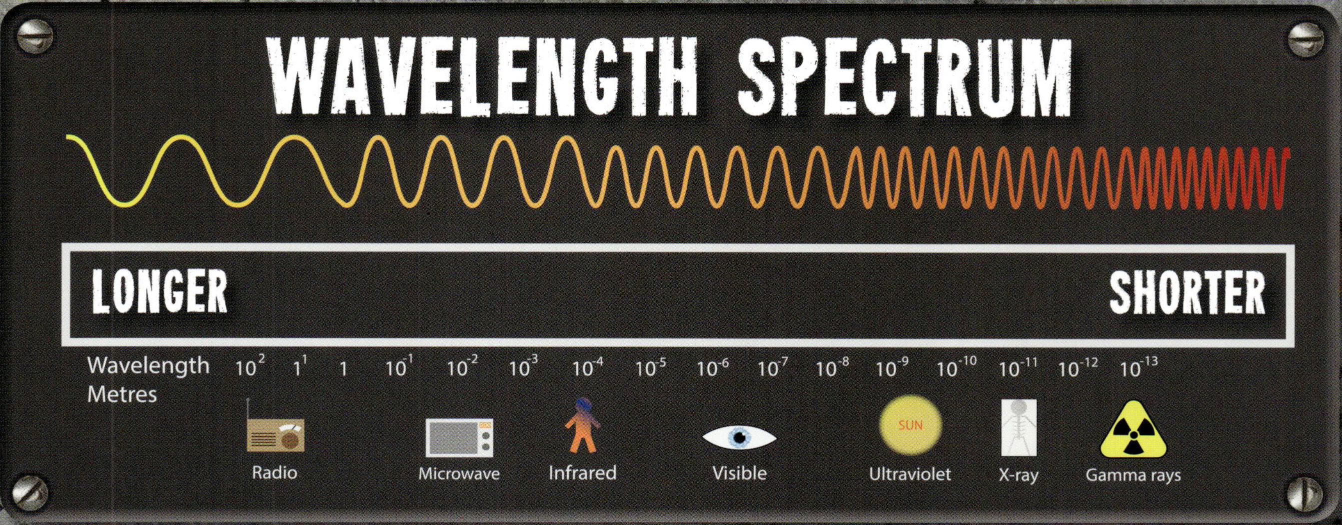

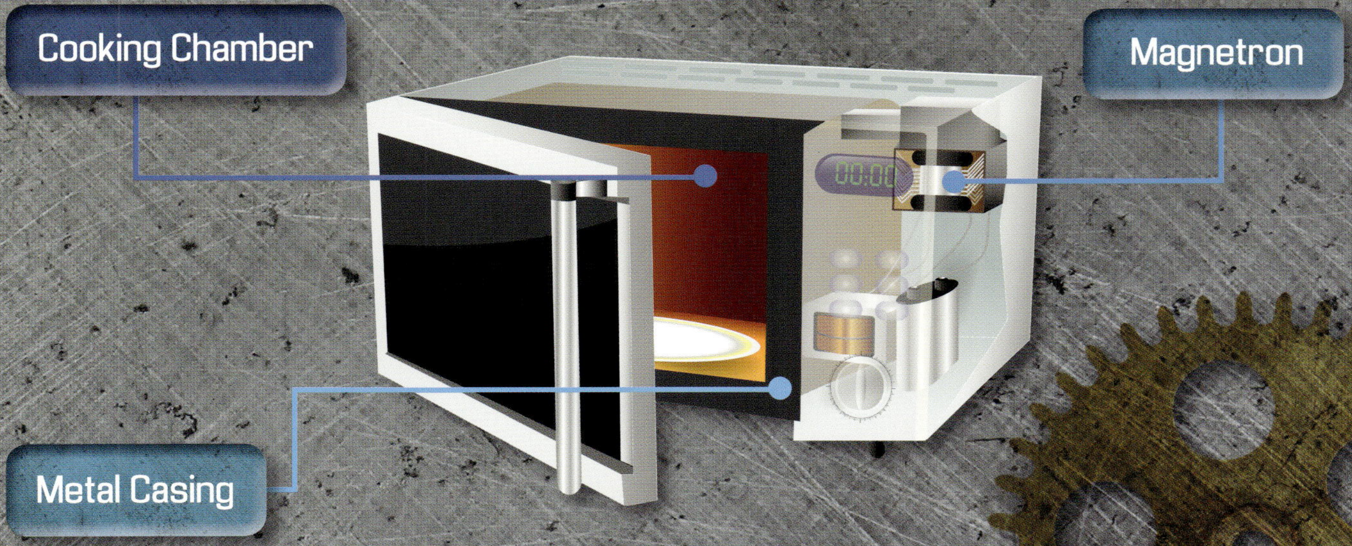

HOW DOES IT WORK?

The microwave oven uses the same technology as a radio transmitter. The radio waves that send television and radio signals are long, invisible waves, but the ones used in a microwave oven are some of the shortest radio waves. Even though they are short they carry a lot of energy.

TEA AND TOAST

There are two small machines in almost every kitchen that we all take for granted: the electric kettle and the humble toaster!

BOILING THE KETTLE ISN'T WHAT IT USED TO BE

The electric kettle is a simple device. When it is switched on, electricity is passed through a heating element which gets hot and heats the water it sits in. Later, a device that switches off the kettle when enough steam escapes was added.

The first electric kettle took nearly 12 minutes to boil!

WHAT'S SO GREAT ABOUT THE KETTLE?

The electric kettle is a real timesaver. It was developed by the British, who are well-known for their love of tea. It is estimated that people in Britain make around 165 million cups of tea every day.

KETTLE THEORY:

Boiling water in an electric kettle is around 193 seconds faster than boiling it on the hob. That doesn't sound like a lot, but considering that the British drink around 165 million cups of tea a day, that soon adds up.

WHAT DID THE ROMANS EVER DO FOR US?

People have been toasting bread since the pyramids were built. In fact, the Romans loved toast. Our word toast comes from the Latin word 'tostum', meaning to scorch or burn. It would seem that people have been toasting bread for thousands of years, but the electric toaster wasn't invented until 1893 – so how were they doing it? The answer is simple: over an open fire.

Toaster, 1920s

A TOAST TO TECHNOLOGY

The first electric toasters would only toast one side of the bread. You would then have to turn it over by hand. They would also set on fire regularly. It wasn't really until the invention of sliced bread that they really picked up in popularity, making toast a go-to breakfast for those in a hurry.

THE BEST THING SINCE...

Have you ever heard someone say that something is 'the best thing since sliced bread'? Do you know what they said when sliced bread was invented? That it was 'the greatest forward step in the baking industry since bread was wrapped'. This was the marketing slogan for the first pre-sliced bread.

People were really worried that sliced bread would go stale before they got it home.

THE MAN WHO BELIEVED IN BREAD

The automatic bread-slicing machine was invented in 1928 by Otto Rohwedder. This machine would go on to change the contents of lunchboxes for ever. At first, people were very sceptical, but Otto knew that he had invented something that would be really convenient for consumers.

This was before preservatives could make food last for weeks.

OTTO'S MARVELLOUS MACHINE

Otto's machine had evenly spaced serrated blades that moved up and down very quickly. These would cut the bread into even slices. Rightly, bakers were worried that it would dry out too quickly, and that was when he had a bright idea. What if the machine wrapped the bread in plastic as well?

Wrapping sliced bread in plastic became the standard for preserving its freshness.

So, the next time you bite into a sandwich or a piece of perfectly-sliced toast, remember Otto and his marvellous machine.

EVER IMPROVING

This basic design has been improved on and something very similar can be found in modern bakeries. Now these machines can be found in factories that produce millions of loaves a day, that are all sliced and wrapped along a conveyor belt.

THE KING OF FROZEN FOOD

Frozen Food Aisle

TRAVELLING FOOD

Today, if you go into any supermarket you will find aisle upon aisle of frozen food. But that wasn't always the case. People had a few methods of preserving food – putting it in tins, or jars, or preserving it in salt. But most of the time, people had to buy food for that week, or sometimes even that day. Let's look at how frozen food has become an everyday staple in many kitchens.

CLARENCE 'CAPTAIN' BIRDSEYE

One man is responsible for changing the way that food was frozen and transported, and that man is Clarence Birdseye. Frozen food was available before Birdseye joined the market. However, Birdseye had realised that the food he froze for his family tasted a lot better than the frozen food that could be bought at the time.

Birdseye didn't invent freezing food, but he did come up with better ways of doing it.

THE SCIENCE OF FREEZING

When food is frozen slowly, at temperatures between -4 and -9 degrees Celsius (°C), it can change the way that cells are held together inside the food. What Birdseye discovered was that he could reduce this cell damage if he froze the food faster.

Clarence Birdseye is a part of the Frozen Foods Hall of Fame.

Birdseye developed a method of flash-freezing by placing the food between two metal plates. These plates were kept at -25°C. Birdseye revolutionised how frozen food was first frozen then packaged, and how it was transported. Thanks to him, we saw frozen meals, TV dinners and, of course, fish fingers become more and more popular!

TRAVELLING FOOD

One of the ways that Birdseye managed to make frozen food so popular and change the way people ate for years afterwards was using refrigerated trucks. But he did not invent them; Frederick Jones did, by creating a portable air-cooling system in 1930 that could be installed in vans. This became Birdseye's secret weapon.

Refrigerated Van

This innovation made transporting fresh and frozen food a possibility where it hadn't been before. We can now regularly eat fruit grown in other continents and have our whole shopping order delivered right to our doors. None of this would have been possible without Frederick Jones' invention. And don't forget about the ice cream vans! We can thank Fredrick for those too.

HOW DOES IT WORK?

First things first – you can't 'make' cold! What you can do, however, is take heat away. Think about it working in the same way as light and the colour black. We only see black when there is no light. Black is when there is no colour. Well, cold is when there is no heat!

ABSORBING HEAT

To remove heat from a space, it must be insulated. This means that it is heatproof. Metal tubes that have a special cooling liquid inside usually wind along one wall. This liquid absorbs the heat from around it and changes into a gas. This gas is then compressed – this means that it is squeezed. Air from outside is passed through it, taking the heat outside with it. The gas then turns back into a liquid.

FOOD FROM THE FACTORY

MACHINES OF CHANGE

The Industrial Revolution changed almost everything about how we live – even the way we eat. Much food production and preparation moved from local butchers and greengrocers into large factories. But what were the machines that helped this happen?

Biscuit Factory

THE CONVEYOR BELT

The conveyor belt is one of the most essential pieces of machinery in any factory – moving things from one machine to another or from one part of an assembly line to the next. It is because of this that modern factories can produce so much, and to the same high standard.

Tortellini Pasta Conveyor Belt

THE EVOLUTION OF THE CONVEYOR BELT

Early conveyor belts were made from wood and leather strips and were moved by hand cranks and pulley systems. They were used to transport farmers' goods onto ships as far back as 1795. In 1804, the British Navy used steam-powered conveyor belts to make biscuits for the sailors.

Early Conveyor Belt

Henry Ford

HENRY FORD AND THE PRODUCTION LINE

In 1913, Henry Ford changed the way that factories worked. By using conveyor technology in his car factory, he spared his workers from having to move their tools from one car to another and, in doing so, saved lots of time. This way of working soon became the standard for factories and is still in use in many factories today.

FOOD FROM THE FARM

MORE PEOPLE EQUALS MORE FOOD

Before food reaches factories, shops and our homes, it often starts off on farms. But how have machines changed the way that farms work? The way food is grown, harvested and transported on farms has been completely transformed by machines. With over seven billion people on the planet, we need to grow a lot more food than ever before. Machines help us to do this.

Machines changed the way we farm.

I'VE GOT A BRAND-NEW COMBINE HARVESTER

The combine harvester is a machine that is used to harvest grain. It gets its name from the three different tasks it does at once: reaping (cutting and gathering), threshing (loosening grain from the stem) and winnowing (separating the wheat from the chaff). Because the combine harvester does so many jobs at once, it reduces the cost of grain-based foods by a huge amount.

GOT MILK

These dairy cows are being milked by machines.

Like many things on modern farms, milking cows can now be carried out by machines. The demand for milk has meant that farmers needed to find more efficient ways to get the milk from the cows. That is where the milking machine comes in. By using a machine, a few farm workers can milk hundreds of cows at once.

Without milking machines, there wouldn't be enough milk to fill the aisles at the supermarkets.

HOW DOES IT WORK?

The milking machine uses pumps to create a vacuum – this is when the air is removed from a container creating a low-pressure area that will suck air or matter in to fill it. By creating this vacuum, the milk is sucked from the teats of the cows and into a large container.

FAST FOOD REVOLUTION

Fast Food Restaurant

EATING ON THE GO

People's lives are busier than ever before. People often need food quickly when they are on the go. That is where fast food comes in. But what makes fast food different? Like the name suggests, it is cooked fast, but it is also consistent. That means it is always the same, even when bought from different locations.

ASSEMBLY LINE COOKING

Like Ford's factory, fast food restaurants use an assembly line system to prepare your food. By using machines that have precise timers and specific temperatures, fast food restaurants make food that is almost exactly the same every time and from every restaurant. This is called standardisation.

These fryers have computerised temperatures and timers, so the staff know when the fries are done.

AUTOMATION

Automation means using automatic machines to carry out a task that would normally be carried out by people. More and more fast food restaurants have been adding automated kiosks into their restaurants – these are self-service stations that take your order for you. This is only possible because of the standardised menu and production method.

Would you rather order at the self-service kiosk or the counter?

HOW HAS AUTOMATION CHANGED THINGS?

The effects of this kind of automation are yet to be seen. Some people are worried that automation will be the end for some jobs, such as cashiers. It is not just fast food that is affected by automation: factories and supermarkets have also seen jobs carried out by humans replaced with automatic machines.

Do you think that one day, all parts of the fast food experience will be automated?

EATING IN THE INFORMATION AGE

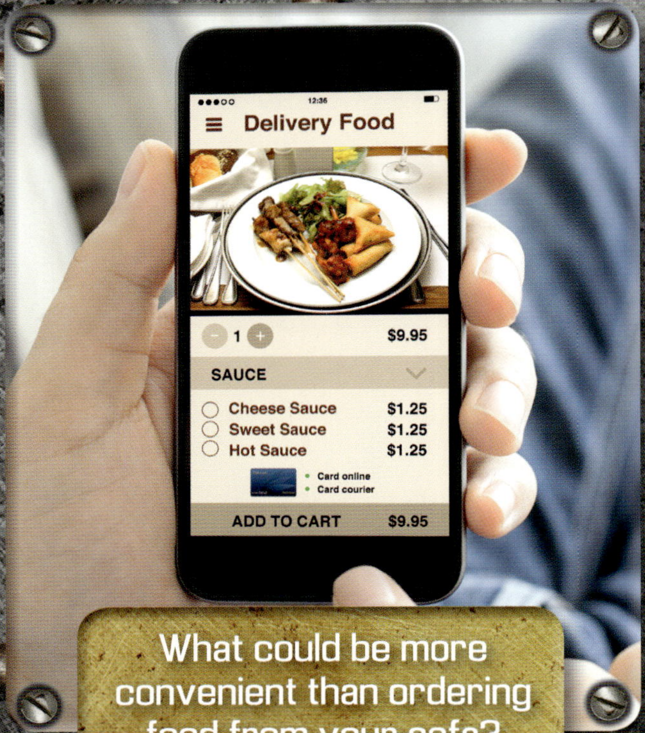

What could be more convenient than ordering food from your sofa?

WHAT DOES IT MEAN?

One machine has changed our relationship with the way we find and make food: the mobile phone. This little device can tell us what foods are good for us, what people around us are eating and let us order groceries and takeaways to our door – all without needing to get off the sofa!

INSTAGRAM

People love to share pictures of their food on the mobile app Instagram. If you search #food, you will find accounts with millions of followers that post images of food they have made and bought. Do you think seeing what other people eat changes how we think about our own food?

Do you think that these people on Instagram only ever eat beautiful food?

ORDER BY APP

The information age is all about convenience, and ordering food has never been easier. By using an app, you can have all of your information stored, making the process much more convenient than before. You also do not need to worry about whether the person on the other end of the phone misheard you because you can input your order using the app.

NUTRITION APPS

Nutrition apps help people to make healthier choices about what they eat. They can calculate how many calories and fats we have each day, tell us which foods are healthier than others and help you to manage your eating habits. Some even use barcode scanners to bring up this information.

Many people always have their smartphones with them, making ordering or choosing food easy and convenient.

FOOD OF THE FUTURE

3D PRINTED FOOD

3D food printing is more than just making pretty sugar sculptures, which it does very well. Pioneers of 3D food printing believe that it will be able to help feed people in places where they do not have access to fresh foods. There are plans for printers that could make familiar foods like pizza and pasta, replacing some of the ingredients with sustainable sources such as algae.

THE ALL-IN-ONE MICROWAVE

A new type of microwave is being worked on that the inventors claim can cook all the different parts of a meal at the same time. It can apparently do this by using sensors that measure the density and moistness of a food and change the radio waves to cook each item separately. They claim that this will mean that it can cook meat, vegetables and bread at the same time with targeted radio waves for each.

GLOSSARY

agriculture	the practice of farming
bacteria	microscopic living things that can cause diseases
billion	thousands of millions
cells	the basic units that make up all living things
chemicals	substances that are usually produced artificially by scientists
commercial	having to do with trade, business and making money
consistent	maintaining the same standards or methods
consumers	those who buy goods or services
continents	very large areas of land that are made up of many countries, like Africa and Europe
conveyor belt	a type of machine used in factories that carries items along a predefined path
cycles	a loop of events that follow each other
demand	to need or require
element	the part of an oven that transforms electrical energy into heat
harvested	the process of crops being gathered
hearths	floors of fireplaces
Industrial Revolution	a period of time from the late 1700s to the early 1800s when technology changed how things were made
kerosene	a liquid fuel made from crude oil
Latin	the language of ancient Rome and its empire
low-pressure	less than the normal level of pressure
marketing	the advertising and activities of selling a product
microwaves	electromagnetic waves with a wavelength between 0.001 and 0.3 metres
moisture	liquid in the form of very small drops
molecules	the small parts that make up everything
potential	possibility or capibility of coming into being
revolution	a complete change in a field or area of production
sceptical	having or showing doubt
serrated	to have small notches or teeth like a saw that help to cut
society	a collection of people living together
species	a group of very similar animals or plants that are capable of producing young together
vacuum	a space devoid of matter

INDEX